Greta Duval

Surviving The Loss of A Pet

A Support Guide to Coping With the Grieving After Losing a Pet

Table of Contents

An Introduction to Pet Loss

In today's impersonal, high-tech, and sophisticated society, more people who never value their pets, considering them as dear family members, dear friends, and confidants. Pets serve many important purposes and play many important roles in our lives and provide physical and emotional well-being. Its presence has a calming effect; blood pressure decreases, as well as loneliness and depression. There are many reasons that are responsible for raising animals, taking $ 36 billion a year.

Pain is a normal, natural, and healthy response to loss, but we rarely socialize to understand and manage this intense emotion. It is quite difficult for us to cry and talk about the loss of a loved one. It is much more difficult and uncomfortable to talk about the loss of a pet. However, for many of us, pets are family members, and psychologists have long recognized that the pain experienced by pet owners after the death of their pet is the same as the pain experienced after the death of a person. In fact, many ordinary people may cry more for an animal than for another or a close relative.

It is often uncomfortable or embarrassing for people to talk about losing a pet. There are no public rituals like funerals and memorials, to console pain. There are so many emotions that they cry for the loss of the experience of pets: isolation/care of friends and family, depression, sadness, uncontrollable crying. Also, anger towards you, vet, or God, guilt that is not doing enough for the animals, care, loneliness, inability to focus or concentrate, depletion of the body, loss of consciousness, and loss of air.

People who complain about the loss of a pet should realize that they are not alone, that many others complain about the loss of a pet. They should understand that pain is normal, natural, and healthy. They should openly and sincerely express their feelings to others who understand and empathize. They can find local support groups and contact their local animal welfare organizations to see if there is any advice.

For many of us who share our hearts and live with animals, we must realize that when these animals die, there is a deep void in our lives. We are used to taking care of our pets and spending quality time with them. They play an important role in our daily lives and activities. When they leave us, we are left alone and lonely. None of us cry this way; there is no time to repent. How long and how we cry will depend on the value and intensity of the relationship we share with our animal companion and the amount of other significant losses we have suffered."

Pain is one of the most difficult, profound, and painful emotions we will experience. Once we learn to recognize and identify our pain, it is important to express it in an empathetic and supportive environment with people who are compassionate and have experienced pain alone. We must read and seek the theme of pain and understand that each of us knows that suffering and pain is an inevitable aspect of life on earth.

Pet Loss Grief

Most of us have experienced the pain of losing a loved animal at some point in our lives, and depending on what relationship we have with our animal, it is undoubtedly possible to measure how much pain we suffer after the loss. Some people create a deep connection with their Pets over time, while others may just enjoy and usually recover quickly from the pain. They can also immediately replace the pet to help with management and get through the grieving process faster. Everyone has their own way of coping with the loss of Pets.

The loss of an individual companion animal can leave devastating suffering, and most people will quietly suffer for fear that they don't take it seriously, just because the loss wasn't a human loss. Today, many people are in situations where their pets mean everything that anyone can do. Many were disappointed by others, so they turned to animals for unconditional love and company, and as a confidant. This is perfectly normal because animals have traits that our human peers don't offer.

Animals have become an integral part of our family, and when an animal dies, we feel like one. I lost my lizard just a year ago, and the pain I felt was so overwhelming that I didn't want to continue. I felt that the best thing I could do for myself and on behalf of my late pet was to write about animal loss and become an "animal loss consultant," which I only started learning about in an online school. The connection I had with my lizard was very deep.

Our Pets, or as I prefer to call them "family," teach us a lot about each other if we let them tell us. Even after reflection, the lessons themselves are brighter and more real. Heartache over losing a pet is not something that can be hidden or shamed. Animals are our family, and we pay for them in this way. There are groups that you can join on social networks like Face book. This allows the grieving pet guardian to express their grief in a safe and unscrupulous social environment

Today, we live in a world very different from what it was twenty years ago; no one should bottle their emotions no longer afraid of ridicule. Accommodation is not classified as "Pets only," but our best friends, and especially our mentors.

The new perspective on animal loss and grief

Do you know that about 63% of all households in the United States have a pet? Some surveys show that there are 75 million dogs and 85 million cats. It's a lot, just love!

Sooner or later, the owners will have to face the impending death of their favorite pet or beloved pet. After the precious "furry baby" has provided unconditional love for years and become part of the family, it's no wonder owners are crying during the pet loss process.

Animals make a much greater contribution to our lives than to business. Animals seem to understand our souls and are our other "children." Owning a pet has many scientifically documented health benefits, in addition to the fact that they teach, inspire, and illustrate many other positive traits.

When the day comes when the "time" for your pet will pass, or tragedy will strike unexpectedly! You have just realized that the pain of the animal, the loss of it, is real and destructive. Your heart is fighting for optimism after losing a pet. If you are wondering, what have I done enough? Was it there for my pet like it was for me? Why now? Your mind is searching for answers, while your heart is in trouble, hurt, and just empty! Make your fur!

So, you read every book about supporting grief for the loss of Pets, every Rainbow Bridge, animal spirit, animal angels book, and all the other inspirational animal books you can find. Then you think about working with animals, animal psychics, intuitive animals, and your mind starts searching for new forms of consciousness through your love for the animals that you have lost. You are deeply wondering if an animal can "come back," and if the reincarnation of animals is real. Can Pets and animals have a past life? And the answer is, yes!

Studying the past life of Pets and reincarnation of Pets will help you understand why your pet changes its body. Your reincarnation education will guide you through the journey of pain, teach you to understand the transition of Pets, death, and the process of rebirth.

Your heart no longer hurts when your friends and family talk: "get over it; it's just a pet!" Or, "are you crazy thinking you can communicate with a dead pet?"

Communication of animals with the living room and the animal is real. Several scientific studies support the link between species.

Although the belief in reincarnation goes back to the Egyptian and Hindu religions and is accepted by the yogic vision, it is only beginning to take on a General consciousness. There are many wonderful resources with real case studies and stories about the reincarnation of Pets. Once you learn about the reincarnation of Pets and animals, your new perspective on the pain process after losing an animal will provide support, comfort, and inspire hope and a touch of vision, rather than eternal tears.

Coping with the Sudden Loss of a Pet

The accidental death of an animal

While many people watch their pets live a long life and then face the loss of their pet in old age, others face the sudden and traumatic loss of a pet due to an accident or negligence. Whenever the loss is sudden, we often feel an avalanche of guilt and questions afterward. Sometimes, this sense of guilt can be obsessive, filling our mind and heart with weight and confusion.

Normal Fault Reactions

Guilt can turn into a real monster after losing a pet. Although the loss of our companions already saddens us, we are also fighting for the accident that took our pet's life. Even when others offer empathy and condolences, we often look for reasons to feel guilty. The "why" becomes part of our thought process. Why did I leave the door open? Why can't I spend more time with him? And "if only," becomes a partner "why" in our destructive thinking. If only I'd paid more attention to him. If only you'd taken him to the vet sooner.

These criminal problems are normal reactions because humans believe in cause and effect. We tend to think that all the bad things that happen can be avoided. As pet owners, we think that in the end, we are a caregiver or protector of our pet. Therefore, the combination of feeling able to prevent the cause of death of our pet, combined with the failure we feel without protecting our pet, creates a lot of guilt. Even if we have friends or family who express their condolences for our loss, it is difficult even to listen to them.

ᴠ guilt can help us

Guilt is normal and sometimes useful because it can often teach us what to do right with our next pet. Overcoming guilt allows us to be stronger and healthier emotionally and spiritually. There are certain things we can do to alleviate the guilt and finally accept the sudden death of the animal and the loss of a pet, caused by pain.

How to cure excessive guilt

We can start without repeating these feelings of guilt, over and over again in our heads. Obsessive thoughts can be huge and, although natural, we do not want them to occupy our minds often. You can recognize this thought, but then follow it with a positive statement. For example: "I feel guilty for Sparky's death. If I'd done that blood test sooner, however, now I choose to heal and move on because Sparky wouldn't want to get caught up in the guilt. I gave him a good home, he loved me very much, and

I will respect that love as I decide to remember and respect our good times together."

Another way to heal guilt is to accept ourselves and realize that there is nothing we can do to go back and change. Fighting for the sudden loss of a pet will not make our pet. Instead, look clearly at what went wrong and make changes that will never happen again. If you have nothing to change, tell yourself that you did everything possible at that time, and in the future, you will strive to always make the right decisions about your pets.

Imagine yourself on the Rainbow Bridge

If you haven't heard of Rainbow Bridge, you can go online and search. Rainbow Bridge is a beautiful image of where you will meet your pet once you finish your time on Earth, and you will move from this life to a monument.

When you meet your pet at that time at Rainbow Bridge, you will not punish yourself or feel guilty for everything you did or did not do for your pet. You will be received by unconditional love. Your favorite pet companion wants to make you feel good and live a balanced and harmonious life. Imagine meeting your pet at Rainbow Bridge now, in advance, and immediately get tips for your life. What do they want from you now in your life, if you try to feel guilty and unhappy?

Balance and forgiveness

Finding balance is an important way to overcome guilt and heal. Balance is important for a healthy lifestyle. Sometimes, when we experience a sudden loss of a pet, we focus only on what happened. However, there have been many more good times than bad, and we need to find a way to focus on those times. Sometimes, a memory diary helps us focus on these moments. Other times, we could go somewhere or do something that our pets would like to remember how we had fun together.

Finally, forgiveness is really the key to healing from guilt. We must learn to forgive past discontent; they're everywhere, and they're made. Sometimes, you may have to look in the mirror and say to yourself, "I forgive you." Your pet's love for you was unconditional, and forgiveness was freely transmitted. When you cry over the loss of your pet, you must forgive yourself.

Fusion with life after loss and guilt

Feeling guilty about the sudden loss of a pet is a natural part of the grieving process. The normal amount of guilt is good for health because it allows us to learn from mistakes and become stronger and more balanced people. If you feel guilt suppresses or captures your life, you can seek help from a counselor or support group. If you cannot find a local Pet Loss Support Group, connect online. There are also a lot of votes against the fall of pets.

Give yourself time to work through your pain, including all the guilt after losing your beloved pet. Be good for yourself. You will feel good again, connected to life, and more compassionate because of your loss.

Pet Loss and Funerals

Losing a pet can be a very difficult task. When an animal dies, you don't just lose one animal; you lose a friend and family member. This is especially difficult when this animal was there for you, day in and day out, and showed only affection and devotion.

They all relate to death in different ways. The most important thing is to understand that it is very normal to experience feelings of pain, sadness, anger, and guilt. It is also extremely important to remember that you are not alone; many people have experienced the death of a friend or family member and have become aware of the feelings you are feeling. Although we all have the same feelings, we all express them differently. Of course, there is no good way to express your feelings; it is important that you express them in one way or another. The worst thing you can do for yourself is to keep your emotions in a bottle. There is no standard period when people feel these emotions; it may take a few days to move forward and a few weeks for others.

Some common ways to express emotion and closure after losing a pet are funeral services or spreading your pet's ashes to their favorite place. Closing and accepting death does not mean that you completely forget about your pet. Many people have decided to create a memorial, photo books, or write gifts and poems about their pets. The loss of an animal is often very difficult to explain to a child, especially if it is their first experience of death. It is very important to include them in creating memories to help them remember all the good times. Five funeral homes can ensure the closure of your family must go through this loss.

Pain support groups and counseling lines are not an uncommon way to express your feelings. Being surrounded by people in these situations can be very therapeutic and remind you that you are not alone. Such support is especially useful for people who are depressed and are experiencing difficulties with the acceptance of death.

It is very important not to get a new pet too soon. You always need to wait until you are ready to fully commit to a new long-term relationship before committing. Don't choose a pet with the intention of replacing your old pet because it rarely works. This is not only unfair to you, but just to a good animal.

Plan a Kid-Friendly Pet Memorial Service

Planning any funeral ceremony for pets is difficult. In the end, it is still shrouded loss of a close friend and companion, and you can hardly understand how to deal with grief, not to mention how to store a pet that means a lot to you. The situation can be even worse when they are involved in children because they have to help manage the loss by facing their pain.

However, planning a kid-Friendly pet memory Service is a way to channel that pain into something positive. While many commemorative pet services designed can be rigorous and simple, allowing your child to insert little children planning, and creative contribution in the process of filling services, can be an ideal way to help overcome the pain for the loss of animals.

When planning a funeral ceremony in childhood, it is important that the child has as much contribution as possible. Ask them to offer great snacks or ideas for food and drinks. You can have a children's dining table and an adult dining table. If you are preparing gifts for pets to your child to help you in the kitchen, make sure that they feel part of the process. As for decoration or wedding, you can assume that your child paints photos of your deceased pet to represent what he or she meant to your family. It's always a good way to prevent pain because art therapy is a positive way to eliminate those feelings.

Buy colorful children's animals and let your child fit into the room or place them where the service will take place. Together, plan to celebrate your pet's life by trying to focus on the good times you've had together, and how your pet influenced your family rather than left.

Invite other children and ask them to come to five funeral services to talk about their pets and why their pet meant so much to them. Or ask some of your child's closest friends to talk about their experiences with a pet when they visit your home. Do not forget that your child emphasizes that it is normal to express the emotions that they feel during a funeral ceremony, both happy and sad.

Keeping a memorial for pets and allowing the child to truly participate in the planning process, teaching them healthy ways to deal with a pet loss pain as children. With age, they will understand positive results, to help them cope with time, death, and these coping mechanisms will be even more relevant if ever they are suffering from the loss of animals. Pet memorials-the perfect way to relieve the pain of the loss of a pet, when he shares it with the world, how much joy your pet has brought into your life and allows the child to be part of this process is one of the best gifts you can give them in this time of trial.

Understanding the Range of Emotions When Dealing With Pet Loss

There are so many different emotions running through your mind and heart when you face the loss of a pet. In fact, the range can be so great that it can really confuse some people. Everyone expects to feel sadness, having just suffered the loss of a pet. Often, however, do not expect to feel the anger, frustration, confusion, and anxiety that often accompany sadness.

The loss of pets can negatively affect how people work day after day, and how they deal with the pain process. Pet loss can be as devastating as any other type of loss. Pets serve as faithful companions to their owners, and their care can be just as frightening as the loss of a close friend or family member.

In addition, this deep emotion which occurs every time there is a loss of this size, is quite normal and is part of the general cycle of pain. Anger and frustration exist because people can't figure out why the death occurred, and how to work through the void left by the loss of their friend. Many pet owners invest so much time, resources, but most of the love and friendship with your pets makes it difficult to let go of one of the most important relationships they had with other living beings.

And depending on the level of spirituality, a person may have unresolved questions and feelings about death in general, which can cause the loss of a pet. Accept that these feelings are normal and come face to face with them, rather than bury them in the depths of my soul. It is really the only safe way to cope with the emotions that come with loss, the destructive of a pet.

In addition, there are many other ways to cope with this loss, including preserving the memory of pets in different ways. Performing a real funeral ceremony or cremation of pets is a step in the process that gives pet owners the opportunity to be close. Then the calendar of the things memorable for pets, the writing of memories online for pets, and even the creation of a beautiful album with photos of many memories left by your pet, this is a healthy method of pain, which can help a person to take the loss of a pet. These are all healthy ways to cope with the pain of losing a pet. For those who suffer from loss of any kind, some consultations can help to resolve feelings about what happened. Still, usually, it is necessary in extreme cases, sadness, and in these situations, the main problems usually occur.

The loss of pets is a serious and destructive event in life, and the work of pain, rather than suppression, is critical. It is as important as the loss of a person who has suffered the loss of a loved one. Pet owners should afford to experience all the emotions associated with such a loss and depend on the support network around them, including family members and close friends. In addition, the memory of the good moments of division between the owner and the pet through the process, the memorial also makes a big difference in the resolution of all the feelings remarkable about this loss and all previous losses, which have arisen in my life.

Significant and Profound Loss or Much Ado about Nothing?

For those who have deeply loved and lost their other creatures, the answer is obvious and still upsetting. There are still too many people in our culture who minimize and trivialize the loss of a pet. They say to a grieving friend, colleague, or family member, "what's wrong with you? Overrun. It was just a dog or cat, bird, horse, etc. Take a new one! Because of all this, you don't need to be so devastated."

As a grief counselor and mediator in a pet loss support group for many years, I have found a wide range of stories about people who have suffered cruel and insensitive statements from others, other people who receive wonderful support and unconditional love from their family, and if you add stress to cope, the process of pain becomes more and more complex.

Animals, like humans, are spiritual beings that have an earthly experience. Many people in my pet loss group recognize these spiritual beings as their teachers and healers. Regretting his physical absence from our lives is not only normal, but also respects his amazing gifts for us. As many of us know, the pain process has no schedules and is unique for every situation and relationship. As a spiritual experience, it offers the possibility of a positive transformation of ourselves and gives us more meaning and purpose in our lives.

Tips for treatment

- Allow yourself to feel all your feelings. It is a sign of strength, not weakness, to feel deeply. Breathing exercises can relax you and allow your senses to move more freely. Writing a letter to your pet can ease the pain in the heart.

- Stay in touch with other people who care about you and understand, as much as possible, your attachment. Be receptive to their kindness and help with everyday activities such as shopping or Laundry.

- Join a pet loss support group to help you through the initial difficult period of mourning.

- Be kind to yourself and give yourself as much time as you need to cry. Develop your mind, mind, body, and heart through hours, books, movies, and friends that soothe and soothe your soul.

- Try to stay healthy through proper nutrition, rest, and exercise. This is difficult to do, imagine what your pet would like to do.

- Respect your partner through a memorial, tree planting, community work, or helping a friend.

- Plan events for days that will be particularly difficult, such as holidays, birthdays, and anniversaries.

- Some depression is a normal reaction to pain. If you feel anxious, have suicidal thoughts or plans, drug problems, or long-term depression, seek professional help immediately. Call the crisis center.

- Balance negative thoughts about yourself with positive thoughts such as: "I did everything I could for my pet."I am a kind and compassionate mentor to my colleagues."

- Go for a walk or interact with nature in one way or another. Healthy nature.

- Don't worry about small things. Let your view of what is really important in life expand.

Pain is a process that affects not only the mind, but also the body, and heart. As a pain consultant, I focus on strengthening all aspects of myself to ensure greater balance and integration of the pain journey. As a creative art therapist, I use various tools of expression and integration that open up new perspectives and depth to the healing process.

Pain is a sacred rite, the door to a loving, compassionate, and purposeful life. Move with the energy of pain rather than fight, and you will discover gifts and treasures that are part of the healing method!

Parents, Children, and Pets

However, another parent recently appeared in the media to discuss their reasons for wanting to make a deal with their children before allowing them to have a pet. Undoubtedly, parents from top to bottom of the earth laugh harshly, as they say, through clenched teeth: "Fortunately, we were there, I tried, we got a t-shirt!"

A contract, however, can be a great idea in principle. Children will first agree to achieve the desired goal. But an animal, such as a pony, dog, cat, or Guinea pig, requires time, attention, and care, and some are more demanding than others.

Sitting down to discuss basic rules and develop a contract helps clarify what it means to live with your pet regularly. Feeding, preparing, exercising, and cleaning cells, water bowls, or trash trays require constant consumption. However, this is the case when the parent becomes the type of retreat responsible for loading the game when entertainment, friends, and other interests become too distracting.

The contract requires both parties to sit together to discuss areas of responsibility, accompanied by a signature after the transaction. This can be a valuable way to focus a child's mind on what is expected of them, with sanctions that they can withstand. Displaying a dedicated contract can provide a continuous reminder, even if the rules start to slide.

Responsibility, caring for others, and showing respect are important for children to learn at an early age. I often hear teachers Express frustration to parents who are too busy or distracted to teach children about discussion, disinterest, and commitment. They complain that parents often allow their children's teachers to do their work for them.

Thus, having children who regularly take care of a pet, even when it rains, is an unpleasant task or a long time is an important lesson for life. The contract can provide a clear reminder of what was agreed upon during the initial enthusiasm and promise to the pet.

And a pet can add significantly to a child's life. There are many stories of children whose mental and physical development has improved significantly after a pet has entered their lives. Benefits can change your life.

Dogs, in particular, do not judge and often persist in their demands, wanting to approach and pay attention, giving unconditional love. Their constant presence allows them to become a loyal and inseparable companion, sometimes becoming their only true friend in life. This can be especially important if your child feels lonely, different, shy, or uncomfortable.

Some children will tell their pet to become their confidant. They can feel comfortable sharing their secrets, telling them of accidents in a family, divorce or death, opening up their boredom about the situation at home, problems at school, and finding it easy to reveal their inner fears, worries, and anxieties.

A pet can be the first experience of a child's death and loss. Going through the death of a beloved pet and learning to deal with it, asking questions, and perhaps a funeral or ritual service can be an important lesson. They study pain and related emotions.

However, if there is doubt about the child's ability to maintain interest over many years of commitment to the animal, it is important to carefully review in advance. Or it may be that a very young child can't fully understand how to handle an animal properly, it would be stupid to treat it or worry about taking care of it and accepting its frustrations. Animals have very few ways to protect themselves; their variants tend to bite, grow, and scratch, which results in the animal being punished.

Education is important and can be useful before you follow the animal path, volunteer at an animal shelter, take the animals to someone else to walk and care for, or even sponsor something exotic at a zoo closer, and then visit regularly. There are also virtual animals that require attention and regularly remind their owner of their presence. The child may soon realize that they are not as interested in having a long-term pet. One of these options may be a more affordable alternative, at least initially.

Children and Pet Loss

Children and pets often create a deep and powerful connection throughout life and share a very special and meaningful relationship. These are the best friends and colleagues who spend quality time with each other, play, train, watch TV and listen to the radio, communicate with friends and other family members, sleep, spend a vacation and even rest together. More and more often, we treat our pets as dear "family members," and children are usually happy to have this non-dangerous and non-military" brother." Children seem to understand that their animal companions love what they are and that they do not have to pretend to be someone who does not want to look or dress in a certain way. Children can be alone.

Children trust and trust their animal companions. They share their goals, dreams, secrets, and secrets, knowing that a pet never betrays or condemns them. Children weaken alertness and express their true feelings with the help of a pet without fear of being rejected, misunderstood, condemned, accused, or criticized. They share most of their lives that they could not or do not want to share with other people.

The loss of an animal is often the first significant loss the child experiences. While a child may lose a relative or a friend, the consequences of such a loss are not as devastating as the loss of a person who is trustworthy, faithful, and unconditionally loved and always "close." Like adults, children are afflicted, and every child is afflicted in his own way and for a while. Some children will be closed or isolated and will become calm and attentive. Others may get angry and "reciprocate." Others will not be able to focus on the task and other tasks. Their pain depends on the depth and intensity of the relationship they have with an animal. This may also depend on the number of previous losses they have suffered. Like adults, children should be encouraged to understand and identify why they are crying and express their true feelings openly and honestly.

Adults should encourage children to talk about their feelings. Adults can offer empathy and support, and can also help children understand that their feelings are normal: that it is natural and healthy to mourn losses of any kind. Keeping funerals or memorials and showing a pet with friends and family is very useful. If possible, it is advisable to be real and specific. Shared reading of books about the loss of pets is also useful. Encourage the child to express his feelings by writing or singing, drawing a pet, or collecting photo albums. The loss of a pet gives parents an excellent opportunity to introduce children to the concepts of birth and death, circle and life cycle. Children should be encouraged to cry, respect, and celebrate the life of their pets and, when they are ready, adopt another wonderful animal companion.

Helping Your Child Get through the Grief

It is always difficult to get rid of the loss of a pet, but it can be even more dangerous for a child. It is often difficult for children to know what happened to their pets, and older children who understand are often cared for. When you need to help your child cope with this loss, you can be a little more difficult. You need to not only help your child cope with this loss, but also do it. And it is natural for the child to cry. To help your child provide the help they need, here are some ideas you can use to help your child overcome this moment of pain.

Encourage discussion about pets

The first thing you can do to help your child through the grieving process of your pet is to encourage discussion about this pet. Let them talk about their pet. You also need to be open to your pet. Ask them to tell others about their pet. Speaking of a pet, they can feel closer to their pet even if it has disappeared.

The pain is open, and talking about a pet can be very useful for children who are grieving.

Publish Your Feelings

Another important thing you can do to help your child cope with the loss of pets is to share his feelings. You need to tell your child that you are also frustrated and feel the pain of loss and sadness. Sometimes the best thing you can do to help your child is to squeeze a few tears together. They will feel as if you are there with them, feeling the same pain that will help them overcome it.

Try to honestly answer the questions

You should also try to honestly answer your children's questions if you are asked to skip a pet. Sometimes, it can be a little more difficult for young children. Think about the age of your children and do your best to give honest and age-appropriate answers. It may not be easy, but honesty can help you survive now, even if it is difficult.

Spend time at your pet's Memorial

Taking time out for your pet is a great idea if you have children crying about the loss of your pet. If you have time to sit quietly in your yard, bury your pet, or put it in a pet crate, a special monument can help your child feel close. When you officially cry your pet, it can help your child go through the process by feeling as if he has time to cry for his pet.

These are just a few ideas that you can use to help your child through the loss of pets with you. Use these tips to help them cope with the loss and make sure you have time to cry for your pet.

3 Tips to Help Children Ages 2-6

For many people, a pet is considered an important member of the family. That's why losing a pet can cause a significant amount of pain in the house. When children are involved, special care should be taken as this is often the initial impact of the child on death.

When you help your child cope with the loss of pets, it is important to understand that everyone (including parents) will be affected emotionally. You're going to have to let your kids know it's okay to cry. Showing their own emotions and pain, it sends the message that the animal is an outstanding member of the family and allows the children to show their sadness and thus begin the healing process.

For children aged 2 to 6 years, the death of your pet will feel like the loss of a friend. A child cannot see death as permanent. They may think that their pet is sleeping or that bad behavior or direct anger towards the animal caused death. Avoiding saying that an animal "slept" or "ran away" can reduce confusion or suspicion. If you say that your pet's body no longer works and the animal does not return, it helps to make the explanation simple.

<u>Three tips could provide ideas on how to deal with the death of a pet with children aged 2 to 6 years:</u>

1) Inform your child's teachers about the loss of the animal in case of a change in behavior.

2) Keep at bay getting another pet until the baby shows the desire.

3) Be open to having as many conversations as possible so that your child can share his emotions and challenges.

Helping the child manage the loss of a pet will require a little more attention; however, children can usually agree that their pet is gone and is recovering from the loss.

8 MYTHS REVEALED

To recover from the pain of losing a pet, many people go through a grieving process, which is similar to the loss of human beings. The feelings of loss are real and can be a deep source of pain in their lives. Many friends of pain find that the pain of a suffering person is disproportionate to loss. Here are ten myths about how to recover from the pain of losing pets:

Myth # 1: People who suffer from severe pain from losing a pet are somehow strange or weak.

Fact # 1: Emotionally healthy people often react strongly to the loss of a beloved animal. It's normal, healthy, and also something to be proud of. It shouldn't be a source of shame.

Myth # 2: The loss of the animal is irrelevant in relation to the loss of human lives, and suffering so deeply devalues human losses as a whole.

Fact # 2: Losing a beloved pet can be as important as losing a close human relationship. They are not mutually exclusive.

Myth # 3: Recovery from the pain of losing an animal, you have to go out and replace the lost animal with a new immediately.

Fact # 3: Every pet relationship is different and cannot be simply "replaced" by another. Before you get a new pet, make sure you are ready for a new pet and the bonding process that will take place.

Myth # 4: You must be strong and cry alone. Do not bother others when it comes to their grief.

Fact # 4: It is always useful when you suffer, if you find someone or a group to help you with your feelings. We're all social creatures, and we need support.

Myth # 5: People tell you to "move on."

Fact # 5: This is typical advice from people who have no idea how they suffer their loss. Try to ignore these people and rely on your own support system.

Myth # 6: You're selfish to sacrifice your pet instead of letting them die naturally.

Fact # 6: Euthanasia is a human way to end the intense suffering of a beloved animal. Prolonging the suffering of the animal in pain is a more selfish act.

Myth # 7: To recover from the pain of losing pets, you need to remove their pain and not stop before it.

Fact # 7: Pain must be treated one way or another or will remain unresolved. You do not need to rule your life, but going through five stages of pain will help you recover from a loss faster.

Myth # 8: The best way to make sure you never have to recover from the pain of losing your pet is to never have another pet again.

Fact # 8: It really is not a solution that all relationships, including pets and humans, have the potential to lose. None of us live, but we must continue to build new relationships throughout our lives.

Emotions Surrounding Pet Loss are So Often Misunderstood

You heard the reaction: "it's just a pet." Does someone from the animal die and undergo an extreme reaction?

Losing a pet is very difficult. When we are tormented by sadness, the world becomes chaos and, interestingly, everyone around us continues as if nothing happened. The world keeps turning, and it's very strange.

Perhaps the animal is sick, and you should make a difficult and important decision. Perhaps a friend or a child needs help after the loss of a beloved animal. There may be a lost animal, and a friend or child must agree with what happened. During this journey through pain, people learn a lot about themselves and others. There will be those who cannot understand the depth of feeling of losing a pet or the love, trust, and determination that people share with their pets. However, it is important that those who suffer from loss be true to their own feelings and do what is best for them.

The therapeutic importance of domestic animals is also known for the fun, love, and friendship that animals can bring. No wonder the loss of a beloved animal is so devastating; they are part of the family and, in some cases, the family. People who do not understand, or who express offensively, should avoid each other until some stronger feelings disappear.

Even animals can mourn their lost families or companions. It may be uncomfortable while you were able to make your way through such a loss, but you can reopen your mind and joy with attention and understanding.

Children can be affected by the loss of a pet differently depending on their age; therefore, it is very important to keep in mind that talking about this issue is of crucial importance for them and the whole family. Teenagers can be quite lustful, but get hurt from the inside, because they can have a familiar pet for many years and are terribly absent. Watch for signs in children of all ages and keep in mind that you will also want to have a step or monument of your pet to help them cry for losses that may be their first experience of losing a loved one.

Loss and pain should be considered a normal, albeit difficult, part of life, as well as an awareness of the processes and ways to overcome sadness: it is useful to lead your life on the right path.

Remember that people who complain about the loss of a pet suffer so deeply because they have the ability to care so deeply. For some people, the recovery of losses strengthens them, and this can be a life experience. I hope that when times are tough, we are with the other kind and compassionate and help those we love and care about to travel through suffering in the best way. Their feelings may not be our feelings, but our job is to help them through their emotions because they work on adoption and a happier heart.

Techniques to Deal with the Guilt of Pet Loss

A second later, a day later, or even years after your pet went to Rainbow Bridge; you can always have annoying questions that cross your mind.

"Have I done enough? Should I have taken it for a second opinion? (FAILURE)

Give you different foods or medicines? (FAILURE)

What if I practiced more? (FAILURE)

Why did I leave the driveway without looking? (FAILURE)

How could I leave the Chocolate where I did? (FAILURE)

Did I give you too many supplements, try too many alternative therapies?" (FAILURE)

My pet will forgive me for leaving her at the vet.? (FAILURE)

After his departure, you are in an empty house, and his death affects you. The pain of losing animals crushes you. If you have a feeling of guilt, it cuts your breath and steals the life force from your soul.

The loss of animal pain can potentially have an impact on people as much as human death. Because the animal's life is so intertwined with ours, they become family members. When we feel that we have failed them before or during death, guilt permeates our thoughts and blocks healing. "Guilt is perhaps the most painful companion of death," said Dr. Elisabeth Kubler-Ross, a specialist in death and human death.

If you feel overwhelmed by the guilt of past events, you may not realize that you have a choice on how to deal with that.

You can choose how you feel.

Choose to focus on the happy moments you shared. How do you do it? Taking one thought at a time and making the conscious decision at that moment that you will not be taken hostage for anything that does not celebrate your pet's life. The form changes your pain into loving and beautiful thoughts.

Choose to do something positive and act. Make a significant contribution that benefits others on behalf of your pet. Volunteer; donate pet food, supplies, or your time in honor of your child.

Continue to the next step. Create a place in your pain for forgiveness. You made the best possible decision with the information you had at the time. What have you learned? Would you make the same choice? How about a friend in the same situation who came to ask you for advice?

The past is over. You don't like to relive disturbing memories full of pain. When an unfortunate memory appears, tell yourself: "the past is the past," to create a healthy image of happy animal memories in your mind. Don't worry about how many times you may need to do this. Hold as long as you are moving forward in your thoughts and your life.

If you are a parent, you are the role model for your children by showing them how to move through pain. Make it a special time for the family to sit together and list all the positive ways that your pet has affected your life, such as giving unconditional love, or being a best friend and teacher.

What do they have to teach you? Perhaps you are grateful for the little things, such as lying on the grass, enjoying a good meal, a comfortable bed, or fresh morning air.

Once you start celebrating your pet's life, you will find that if you still miss them, the lacrimation pain of the intestine will weaken. Smile more when you look at Old Photos. Then, one day, you can think about adding another pet of fur, feathers, or fins to your family. This will be because your previous pet opened the doors of your heart and can now welcome another beloved animal that needs it.

Yes, your pet may have disappeared, but its essence will always be with you. That lessons and love shared because Love Never Dies.

Supporting Our Grieving Children to Cope with Katrina and Other Losses

Children may feel the same feelings when they are hurt as adults, but their responses may be very different. In addition, every day through the media, images of death, loss, pain, and violence are presented not only in the eyes of adults, but also in the vulnerable eyes and hearts of our children. Adults barely have the tools and experience to process what they see intellectually and emotionally. Imagine being the youngest and most vulnerable among us to handle this!

In addition, children are deeply affected by natural disasters such as hurricane Katrina. Not only should children who have encountered this storm be immediately considered, but those who are safe in their homes elsewhere in the country should also be treated carefully. Because few people have maps or experiences related to issues seen in other people's lives, and because many parents feel bad about guiding their children through trauma such as Katrina or the death of a loved one, the change is frightening.

However, if adults can't find a way to cope with the changes, how can our children move on with their losses and changes?

Loss and pain cause internal and external changes throughout our lives, but in a way that we can lead. We can learn to use the energy of change to bring not only healing, but also promote integrity in being a child's physical, mental, spiritual, and emotional state.

Let's see how parents can help children cope with death, loss, and pain, whether at home or away.

Working with a shared experience

All children find the pain and changes that relate to them differently, but some feelings and experiences are common to almost everyone.

Children, for example, do not understand the changes around them intellectually, but feel the changes in their life situations physically, emotionally, and spiritually. To help children channel the energy of change, give them peace of mind through their touch. Talk about what happened. Continue to consistently support the procedures that you know. In most cases, they should know that they can count on your support to keep them safe and take care of your needs.

Support for young children in crisis

When it comes to the idea of death, young children and young children under the age of five do not understand the concept of permanence. They repeatedly ask when the deceased will return. Children of this age learn through repetition and play, so they need to patiently tell them over and over again what happened.

Many people mistakenly use phrases such as" disappeared," "rest," "sleep," and "gone to the sky," which can confuse and frighten children. It's better to be honest with them as much as possible. Include them in most processes as you care about participating.

Children come and go from trouble at a pace that accompanies their inner needs. If you notice that you are deviating from behavior, it means that you are likely to benefit from more, not less, structure, including robust routines. They also provide various game materials, such as paper and art supplies, clay, or dolls. Help them use these materials to solve their feelings and thoughts.

Support for older children

Children between the ages of six and ten begin to understand the constancy of death, but they don't want to admit it.

Like younger children, they may want to learn both literal and physical facts about diseases, corpses, and body removal, although they will not search for it directly. It is important to be honest and simple in explaining the details. Again, find out "where I am" in your understanding of the situation. When this is done, give them all the information they need.

When in adolescence, children are in a place of transition of understanding and expression. Peer pressure has begun to strengthen their heavy heads; the internal struggle for independence and vulnerability continues.

These children experience a lot of mixed emotions, and their feelings of pain can certainly be confused. Giving them honesty, support, and "space" to process the changes themselves is important. You can give a diary corresponding to an aged book or a peer support group, if you are open to it.

Working with Mature teenagers

As teenagers mature, their ability to cry with their immediate families usually decreases. They tend to accept their feelings and concerns about their peers or trusted adults, such as a pastor, teacher, or uncle. They may exhibit more acting or risky behavior than younger children. As with other age groups, it is important to be honest, show your feelings and vulnerability, and provide a lot of love and support.

Guilt, a heavy emotion at any age, can be especially noticeable in mature adolescents. Look closely to see if they are related to guilt with the pain they feel. Give him the peace that all your feelings are normal. First of all, let them know that they did not cause a loss. Even very young children may have the idea that they somehow caused the event that led to the loss.

Every child is unique

This summary points to some general differences in development in children who suffer from different age groups. However, because each child is unique, the understanding of death and grief varies from one child to another.

Remember that pain is not a disease; it is a normal response to loss. And most children go through their painful journeys without any major problems. But when the pain is complicated by factors such as family dependency, traumatic death, a history of abuse, multiple losses, and minimal family or community support, children can seek professional help. In addition, the pain of the broader community, as a nation that focuses on the effects of hurricanes, presents additional mixed emotions. Include the child in a discussion about what they see on TV, what their peers and teachers have said about events, and, most importantly, what the child thinks and feels. Ask questions without trying to "do better."

If the child is suffering from destructive behavior, persistence, depression or prolonged abstinence, somatic disorders, weakening or excessive anger, contact a specialist with pain. In fact, these recommendations address any loss, whether it is death, displacement, separation, divorce, or a serious health problem.

Be sure to talk to them

Pain is a problem that is often avoided or treated with fear and pain. As a parent, educator, and counselor, I encourage you to talk to your children about your loss or what you see in the media. Discuss what changes will result in your life due to the death or event of a loved one in the world as much as possible. By providing a structured education, children will learn to deal with future losses and crises with confidence rather than fear.

Also, be sensitive to cultural differences when it comes to death and other losses. Remember that there is never a "way" to learn or do anything

Take care of your needs

In your role as a teacher, counselor, or parent, it's easy to ignore your needs. Of course, she feels real concern for the well-being of children who are facing severe loss, but her feelings about life-changing events are just as important as your own. If they are not allowed to continue, it will be a less effective role model for their children.

In particular, take time to deal with the discomfort when you talk to your children about death and pain. If you know about unresolved pain issues from the past, find a reliable person to talk to about your feelings. Look at this as a great opportunity to do a little "interior cleaning."

Tools and tips

Here are some ideas to help you:

1) Breathing exercises go a long way to reduce loss and change stress. Inhale . . . expire . . . Oh.

2) Remember that it's good to show the children that you also suffer. Recognize their confusion, anger, or sadness about the situation; this gives them permission to feel and cry for themselves. When you show children how to take care of themselves in difficult times, they learn ways to validate life to cope with the crisis and change.

3) Ask the children to tell their stories. They can do this with words, images, or art. You will find that healing is about telling your stories and witnessing the stories of others.

4) Ask the children to finish the prayer and then discuss what happened. For example: "I wonder what it is," or "I'd like to," or "I want you to know," or "the hardest thing for me in my life."

5) It is important to remember that children are not alone. A lot of help is available. Encourage them to think about all the things and people they consider to be their resources. Then ask them to draw a picture or map of these resources with pencils, cakes, pencils, and markers. This card can contain activities and favorite people, pets, even spiritual helpers. It becomes a valuable reminder and a symbol of where they can turn when they feel overwhelmed.

6) Due to the circumstances, sometimes, children do not have the opportunity to say goodbye to their pets when they die. It's hard for someone to cry without being able to say goodbye. Ask your children to write a letter to a pet or missing person, or ask them to say "goodbye" if they cannot write.

7) Encourage your children to draw their feelings or create a collage that represents death, loss, or change. Perhaps they prefer to write a song about death, compose music or compose a sensual dance.

8) When you are grieving, it is important to balance the sadness, anger, and fear you feel with the thoughts of the good things in your life. The same applies to children. Ask them to list everything they feel happy about.

9) Convince your children that children directly affected by the hurricane have loving adults who help and control them. Let them know that you will do everything in your power to protect them and that you have a plan in case something unexpected happens. So make sure you have a plan.

10) Sometimes children feel bad during big changes and losses. Let me make a collage of what it means to be human. Encourage them to show positive and

negative feelings, as well as behaviors that help them see what a "holistic person" looks like. It's about how everyone grows and learns as a result of change.

11) Children, like adults, are often afraid of what awaits them. It is easier to recognize and work with fear when they can "see" rather than trying to hide it. Let them sculpt their fears with clay or other materials.

12) Help your children understand that they have choices about what they think and say, how they react and behave. To reinforce the idea that this choice determines what they get for life.

13) Children and adults feel helpless in situations beyond their control. Our natural inclination is that we want to help those in need. Let your children help you in some way. This will give them a sense of

usefulness and help them develop compassion. Ask them if they have ideas, and if not, they can give suggestions: collect donations from friends, family, at school or in the neighborhood; make bags with the necessary items; they can also write a personal support note that will be included in each bag; organize a fundraiser; collect donations to save pets; hire teammates to write songs, letters, drawings, songs, etc. that they show the love, light, and hope given to the victims and their families with their prayers.

Listen Carefully

When you are with grieving children, your main source is a good ear. This does not necessarily mean your physical ears; it also includes your emotional, mental, and spiritual ears. Deep listening helps you stay close to them and capture their signals. This is a long way to healing for all concerned.

Be careful. If you simply "pursue" them with your knowledge of the grieving process and impose a "mourning," you risk losing confidence due to bad weather. Know that with good tools, your ability to listen to children, and your intuition, you will be guided to help them get a positive and even transformative experience.

Pet Loss & Depression

Are you lonely, sad, and depressed due to the death or loss of your pet? These feelings of pain and anxiety are perfectly normal, but you can rest again. Do you think your pet is a member of your family, your closest friend, and a constant companion?

If you or someone you love have pets, there will be a great sense of loss when that animal dies, flees, or falls asleep. Every day with our pet is special and brings joy to the owner and owner (sometimes it is difficult to determine who it belongs to, okay?

Five ways to relieve pain

It's never just a "way" to heal you from a traumatic blow in your life, but here are some tips that worked for me and others that I recommended during pain workshops. I know because not only have I had some deaths of relatives and dear pets, but I have also volunteered at the hospital and a lot of pain.

Do not let others tell you what you need to feel or reduce your feelings so that others feel more comfortable.

Write your feelings in a newspaper or song.

Make a monument and a gift to your friend; maybe plant a flower or a tree in memory of your dead.

Find a support group in your area or online

Give yourself some time. You have a deep heart rate, and you need a little time to heal yourself.

Do you feel like you just lost your closest and most faithful friend?

Your pain from losing a pet is very real, but I hope these tips will help relieve heart pain. I know pets aren't just animals. They are our closest friends, our permanent companions, and our family members. They form an unconditional love and teach us to be better people to meet them

Ask for help if you need treatment

If you think that the pain, depression, and sadness you feel are just obstacles that you have to overcome, you are wrong. You shouldn't do it alone; there are others who understand your pain.

Let's be honest; no one wants to waste time on sadness, and loneliness. But we all have to go through this at some point in our lives. The fact is that there are ways to go through the grieving process that helps us heal ourselves, also allows us to respect and maintain the memory of those we have lost while strengthening our strength and well-being.

Pet Loss Prevention

Most people love their aquatic animals just like traditional animals and can feel the loss of this type of pet so deeply. After all, while fish and lizards do not necessarily hug and do not play, they bring a certain amount of peace and quiet to the house. Because you invest time, energy, resources, and money to care for your aquatic animals, it is important to care for them as effectively as possible to preserve their life for as long as possible and avoid having to write a memorial for your pet. Although they offer a different type of business, they are still a kind of companion.

Proper care procedures are necessary for the longevity of these animals. Here are some tips on how to properly care for your aquatic animals to ensure a longer life for these fun and colorful animals.

They often clean up their habitats: each aquatic animal needs a different type of habitat. For example, some lizards need semi-dry and heated space; others need strict temperature control and access to more water than others. Snakes need space to climb and hide when they feel threatened. Depending on the type of aquatic animals, you need to know exactly what you can do to ensure that your environment is clean and structured to resemble a natural habitat as much as possible.

If you have a snake, lizard, or other aquatic animals (except fish), look for a veterinarian who specializes in this type of care. Many people make the mistake of thinking that aquatic animals cannot be taken to the veterinarian; it could not be further from the real. With the exception of fish, all animals should consult a veterinarian when they are ill, or annual welfare visits. When choosing a veterinarian for your snake or lizard, be sure to choose someone who has in the past, successful care and treatment of these animals. In addition, the doctor you choose should be patient and be ready to explain exactly what you should do to provide proper care to your pet.

Do your research on the types of health problems these types of animals may face understanding what health problems each specific animal faces can help you understand how to better care for them. Read and search online to make sure you are informed of your pet's specific species. Find information about habits, possible diseases and/or infections, mating habits, parasites common to your pet's species, and more.

The key to Preventing Pet Loss in aquatic animals is to put together as much and the best information possible. Understanding your internal operations and exactly what they need, make sure you are the best possible owner. Also, if you are experiencing loss of aquatic animals, do not feel that your pain is invalid, seek pet loss support from like-minded people who understand what you are doing.

The Importance of Good Bird Health

Anyone who has had a bird for a long time understands how important it is to actively participate in the promotion of good bird health. Even beginners quickly learn that there is a lot to learn when it comes to caring for a bird. There are several ways you can be willing to take care of your bird to try to prevent premature loss of pets.

The priority in ensuring good bird health is finding a respected bird doctor. This type of veterinarian should specialize in birds and fully understand the range of diseases and conditions they may have. Ask other bird owners to make recommendations and schedule consultations/interviews with multiple doctors before deciding on one. A good bird doctor will closely follow all the care of your bird and will take the time to meet your pet. They will look at your entrance and guide you in the right direction when it comes to taking care of your bird.

Therefore, it is important to research the health of birds and some potential diseases and pests that you may have to deal with at some point. Common pests of birds include nematodes, ticks, and some varieties of fungi. Exotic birds should be treated differently from domestic birds, and each bird has its own set of genetic problems. That is why it is so important to examine in detail which birds you have, as well as ask various questions to the breeder or the person who provided you with the bird. Understanding a bird's past and its parents' medical history is the best way to plan potential health problems for your poultry.

According to Pet Bird Magazine, there are several common feathers and skin diseases affecting birds of all varieties, including feather cysts, baldness, dust mites, and feather behavior, which is typical of birds that tend to be emotional creatures. If you think your bird may have any of these problems, do research and make an appointment with your doctor to discuss possible treatments and/or character changes.

Maintaining good bird health is a lifelong commitment. Birds tend to live so long and sometimes longer than humans when they are well-groomed. You should have a plan to take care of your bird, including appointing someone else to take part in taking care of your bird if anything happens to you.

Do You Need Pet Loss Counseling?

So, you are devastated by the loss of a family member, which is your dear pet, and you feel like you need tips on losing Pets.

You may be confused by the depth of sadness in losing a pet. After all, this is "just an animal," Isn't it? We know with you that it was much more than that. First, you must understand that you have the right (and need) to cry deeply and completely about the loss of your pet.

Right now, your grief and yearning for loss have forced you to seek help (or you wouldn't be here). But first, we'll look at some basic truths about the pain of losing Pets that can help you understand and feel a little better.

One of the best things you can do to help yourself is to understand that while most strangers don't understand it, you are fully justified by your deep feelings of pain and loss. Losing a beloved family pet can be devastating. As a rule, our society does not recognize the meaning of losing Pets or allows an adequate fight. You also feel awkward or uncomfortable expressing your pain to others, and you end up feeling isolated and alone in your pain. When an animal dies, there are no official or public rituals, such as funerals, where pain can be expressed openly, and emotional support is freely provided. Since we don't know how to properly manage the pain of losing Pets, we usually suffer in peace.

Now, how do you deal with people who don't understand what you're going through?

These are three biggies that you will definitely hear:

"It was just an animal."

"Just get over it" or

"You can always get another pet."

These statements, which are often heard by well-meaning friends, demonstrate a profound lack of understanding and empathy for their pain.

They just don't understand and probably have never suffered the pain of losing a beloved animal. The best thing you can do is forgive them for their ignorance. They are really bad. Let insensitive comments come out of your back, and don't let them feel like you don't have a legal right to cry. Avoid these "friendly" people and communicate with someone they have found that you care about, and they will hear your painful story without trying to "fix everything."

If you have found your way to this article, look for more help in dealing with pain and perhaps, even tips on losing Pets. And in extreme cases, we recommend professional help. But before we move on to this important (and probably expensive) intervention, we think you should try to find the necessary support among your friends and family.

First, armed with certain knowledge and understanding of the normal process of pain. Find out what reactions you can expect from pain, and learn how to make the pain more bearable. Visit your public library, bookstore, or pet supply center, and request information and literature about the loss and mourning of animals.

It is important to find a clear and unbiased listener who listens to your story and allows you to overcome your pain without providing "quick fixes." It takes time to come to terms with your loss, and it will be easier if you can find a friend to support.

If you feel that you need advice on pet loss to overcome the pain, make sure to schedule an appointment with a pain consultant. You can also find someone who is experiencing the pain of losing Pets. Remove the yellow pages and start calling vets in your area or calling your local pet shelter. Ask if they know any of the five pain consultants. Or call your family doctor and ask for a pain consultant.

Grieving for a Pet with Guidance and Counseling

For many of us who have pets, losing to death is as devastating as losing a family member or best friend. People who do not have a pet tend not to "get it," but those who really understand the deep sense of loss. Our pets are often members of our family, so when we lose them, we experience great pain.

Why do we love them so much?

Pure love and depth of relationship we can have with our dog, cat, rabbit, it is real, and the love that we get out of them is unconditional. In fact, how often have we heard something like, "I'd like for my partner/friend/parent to have unconditional love for my dog." It is clear that the simple nature of the relationship with the animal can cause even more destructiveness when death comes.

Everyone cries differently:

Like the death of a person, we all experience pain and loss in different ways. We can be watery or emotionally bad, or we can feel anxiety, nervousness, or even physically ill. Susan Dawson, a psychologist, and expert in relationships between humans and animals, said: "it is useful to know that some of us are emotionally (emotionally) sad, and our pain is obvious to others. However, some of us feel instrumental sadness and leave their emotions alone, instead of focusing on tasks such as ordering cremation or burying a pet."

Repentance is not a linear process:

We could also experience pain differently on different days; once wrong, another denied that our pet really disappeared. This new pain may lead to further losses which we have suffered in our lives, and if we do not treat them emotionally, the loss of our beloved animal can induce a new sensation of pain from the loss of the elderly.

So what is important to know about the process of grieving for a pet?

- Surround yourself with people who understand your love for your pet and can maintain space through loss.
- Instead, stay away from people who don't understand your loss, so you don't need to explain what you're feeling.
- If you decide to let your pet go, ask your veterinarian if he wants to come to you, if it seems right.

Remember that everything is in order, wherever you are: there is no "good" or "bad" way, how to cry, but keep it under control, it may be harmful to your health in the long term

New Thoughts for Pet Loss and Grief

Finding someone who understands the loss and sadness of pets, as well as what you are going through, can be difficult. Experts recommend that people join groups led by a veterinarian or a person trained in the problems of pain and loss of pets. They will find comforting and useful information about the symptoms and reactions to the loss of pets and the recovery of pain.

The next stage after the first stage of "denial" is "acceptance," where falls and overflow are characteristic of the sadness of pets and those experienced by most people.

Writing a pet day can help you accept the loss of a pet and start coping with the pain.

A pain counselor, especially, can help you navigate the pain path. Unfortunately, in our society, the pain of pets is not considered a "real" form of pain, so, people often feel shame or are shamed for the depth of their pain and sadness. Like "anger," this stage of "acceptance" is a very incomprehensible, but necessary step to restore inner pain. Experiencing the sadness of pets with a counselor can be a healing process for all of you.

Monument

There are many sites that offer community forums. Think about making a memorial for your pet when you feel it's time. The beauty of the monument provides the comfort of a long-term memory.

Or unforgettable animals on these objects give viewers a sense of community.

Or create a memorial for your pets from a variety of objects and photos. Add a nice collection of sad poems about the loss of your pet with memorable poems about pet verses and pet verses.

Or the beauty of the monument guarantees the comfort of a long-term memory. They grew up from an ancient and more traditional system of preservation of cremated bodies in Memorial urns.

On cremation of jewelry becomes the latest trend in many unforgettable traditions. Jewelry pet memorials are in the form of urns or lockets that can be worn around the neck or in the form of a key, worn on a bracelet, or even used as a "pendant scary."

Another strategy

Or change your schedule to fill the time spent on your pet.

Or create a memorial as a photo collage; and talk to others about your loss.

In addition, many online animal loss forums contain a commemorative page for animals in which the owners suffer their loss; owners can pay tribute to their lost animal in the form of paintings, poems, or remains. You will find articles and information about the sadness of pets, seek support, take final measures, and keep the memory of your favorite pet.

Whether you choose pet cremation or pet burial, you will find many companies to help you plan the final burial of your pet's body and keep it for years to come. A memorial for pets can help all family members cope with the loss of a beloved family member.

Finding an urn or homemade items for your pet's creamy powder is much easier when you know what is available and where you can buy it. Create a memorial for your pet from a variety of objects and photos.

As expected, Challenger, IE 28 January 1986 years so wonderfully immortalized by President Reagan, these precious souls have rejected the dark bonds of the earth to touch the face of God.

There are many options for storing the memory of your beloved pet.

About 100% cotton photo blankets

Or engraved glass memory cubes

Or Custom Pet Art

Information about Black Granite Photo markers grieving support-locate links to information about Pet Loss sites and tips for pet loss, which will help you say goodbye with your favorite pet.

Most pet cemeteries, members, and non-members of MAAP celebrate Pet Memorial Day with special ceremonies, open days, and other events. Recently, we have seen a growing need for pet memorials. Usually, when an animal dies, there are no funerals or monuments; often, friends and family do not understand the depth of loss they suffer.

Ask a Really Tough Question: Is Your Pet Loss Grief Support Group a Positive or Negative Experience?

Support groups for pet connections through Angel animals, animal spirits, pet networks, the Beyond of animals, and Rainbow Bridge residents are available in all sizes and flavors. In person, in health facilities, in Church, in homeless animal shelters, does your pet loss group meet the criteria of a positive or negative experience?

A positive, proactive support group is a group that encourages learning. This group promotes progress and contributes to greater awareness and empowerment. I am a blessing in your life!

The leader of the positive group is not intimidated by his unanswered questions, but inspired to be more polite. This moderator encourages you to ask questions that require more research to challenge each member of the group to think beyond the current pet loss "was" circumstances and in a broader mindset of "is it possible that my pet can reincarnate?"

This open-minded attitude discourages group members from maintaining a victim mentality "my pet is gone forever."

A positive animal grief group is aware of the psychological reasons why it can use its negative reaction for "sympathy care." They understand that this is a confusing and complicated moment in your life. However, an animal grief counselor will try to rebuild a new consciousness through uplifting approaches to coping with his life without his beloved animal companion. The work of the moderator is to facilitate his movement through this period of emotional pain and loneliness, not to allow self-pity.

From his introduction "pet loss story," to his weekly "How Are you" story of unhappiness, the negative Animal Loss Support Group comes together solely to celebrate the identity he has created since his pet's devastating death. It is a group of "victims," a connection with others, and a commitment to perpetual negative energy at the highest level of disguise.

No matter how much you think this group will help you cope with the death of a pet, they are not. They exist to talk and share negative experiences creating a "stuck" atmosphere. It's related to the tranquilizers in progress. You do not get points for being a victim of the loss of your pet. In fact, you contribute to your own death.

It should be a great concern to participate in a group that says only what "was," and all the continuous unhappiness that permeates the lives of its participants with the loss of pets. Inevitably, this will have a negative impact on the minds and minds of participants. The details of the death and suffering of your pet do not need to be addressed again and again.

Since you have already experienced your pet loss "history," why should someone continue to activate this pain and negative energy? This is a common scenario on the Internet of groups. Research shows that telling your Horror Story and reading the countless painful breaths of others does not facilitate positive mental responses.

Acceptance is one thing, and denial is another. Being the "victim" of your dead pet drains your energy. Experiencing the loss of pets and coping with it with the "pity poor me" approach is useless. You can get help for a while, but the key here is "for a while." Renounce the feast of pity. Look for a new perspective of pet loss pain to restore your heart and inspire hope.

As long as you say what "was," you live in the past. I know people who always tell the same story about the death of "Fluffy" with every little detail embellished to the fullest just to keep the conversation dynamic with the drama of what it was.

For this type of person, who actually moves after their "oh no" mourning, this animal keeper should have a life and do something more than talk about themselves and their loss.

This type of individual does not move from one person to another, a support group to support group until this group of listeners does not ask enough questions, or provide "poor you, you have lived so long with the death of your pet" comments.

I know of a woman who, after years of mourning pet loss advice and therapy, and ten years in each Pet Loss Support Group, grief pet community sympathy, and pet loss chat room sympathy, she was able to find, Started Her Own Pet Loss Support Group.

Do you have Trends up there? Do you like the attention that facilitates your pain? If so, then you need to determine "why" you need this form of negative attention. This inner emptiness will erode your soul and, eventually, your health.

Do not use the fact that you have lost your pet as an identification marker or to give meaning to your online life.

By creating your identity as a victim who suffers from the death of your pet, you are the only one to lose friends, the respect and patience of those who encourage and support your healing.

Many members of the Animal Support Group want attention. They use their pet's worst illness and death events as a banner to distinguish them. It is imperative that these people have the courage to break with their need to rely on the loss of their pets to give meaning to their life in the "el" group. It's not productive. If a person continues to wallow in this oppressed existence, he can be sure that fewer and fewer people and friends will ask, "How do you feel?"

You can tell the story of your pet's loss as a "learning opportunity" to help educate and heal others in your group, rather than as a compassionate patch. If your group does not continuously support your positive emotional and spiritual growth, leave.

A negative support group ultimately does more harm than good. While pain takes time, uplifting attitudes are essential. Living with the "memory of death" of your pet can drain your energy day after day and breathe after breathing.

I understand that since my boyfriend died in a sudden car accident, I've never had the opportunity to say anything or have a warning.

It is better to celebrate the life of your fur baby and remember all the good times. So keep the positive contribution of the living animal in your life.

By celebrating the life of your pet, you will never have to bury his memories. You can take them out of the memory area of your heart, at any time, as a special gift and savor all the beautiful thoughts and feelings.

Next, analyze the dynamics of Your Pet Loss Support Group to determine if you are growing or just remodeling to the maximum pet loss you have already experienced.

Ask:

1. Does your group adopt an open mind and greater awareness?

2. Do you take the knowledge gained by your group as a positive educational experience?

Unless you choose to grow up, you will remain in the same state as the one that brought you to the group in the first place.

3. Do you stay too long in the pain phase?

4. Do you feel better today than yesterday?

The last but not the least! Have you ever considered that your pet should not live forever as an angel animal, or Rainbow Bridge resides in the animal spirit or beyond?

Kind reader,

Thank you very much. I hope you enjoyed the book.

Can I ask you a big favor?

I would be grateful if you would please take a few minutes to leave me a gold star on Amazon.

Thank you again for your support.

Greta Duval

Printed in Great Britain
by Amazon